THE ONLY SOLUTION TO CAPITALISM VS COMMUNISM

During the 1900's, my great grandfather Mr Leong came from Southern China to Malaysia in search of opportunity

Here, he made a living as a butcher, worked hard and saved up to finally open a hardware store somewhere in the state of Pahang

The reason why he chose the hardware business is because hardware keeps its relevance for a long time and does not spoil with time

As the years went by, he expanded his hardware store business to having multiple chains stores throughout Peninsular Malaysia

Eventually he sold off his chain stores and used the money to buy a very large piece of paddy land somewhere in Southern China

The land he bought even included a mountain which is a tourist spot till this day

This accumulation of wealth took him one lifetime

The farmers who farmed great grandfather's land gets 30% share from the land's harvest

In the 1940's, the Communists took over China. My great grandfather's family, had to flee because they were land owners

Land owners who remained in China during this time were tortured and killed by the Communists

My grandparents fled to Malaysia and became citizens of this land

Hello world,

Today is June 2020, and I, Eugene Leong call out to you from Malaysia =)

THE WORLD BEFORE COMMUNISM

This was the world before the emergence of Communism

Drawing From Leo Tolstoy's book, the Kingdom of God is within https://www.gutenberg.org/ebooks/43409

(Paraphrased due to Russian to English translation & lack of Context, the full context of the story can be found in the link above)

On the estate of a rich landowner, upon a piece of ground held by him in common with the peasants, a forest had been allowed to grow. (When I say that the forest "grew," I mean that the peasants had not only planted it, but had continued to take care of it.) They had always had the use of it, and therefore looked upon it as their own, or at least as common property ; but the landowner, confiscating it entirely to himself, began to cut down the trees.

The peasants lodged a complaint. The judge of the lower court pronounced an illegal decision in favor of the landowner. The higher courts, as well as the Senate, although they could see that the case had been unfairly tried, confirmed the decision, and the forest was awarded to the landowner, who continued to fell the trees.

But the peasants, believing it impossible that such an injustice could be perpetrated by the higher magistrates, refused to submit to the decision, and drove away the workmen sent to cut down the trees, saying that the forest belonged to them, and that they would appeal to the Czar himself before they would allow it to be touched.

The case was reported to St. Petersburg, from whence the Governor received the order to enforce the decision of the courts, and in order to execute the command, asked for troops.

Hence these soldiers who, armed with bayonets and provided with cartridges and rods expressly prepared for the occasion goes on their way to enforce the decision of the higher authorities. The execution of an order from the ruling powers can be accomplished either by threats of torture and death, or by the enforcement of those threats, according to the degree of resistance on the part of the people.

If the peasants resist, the result is as follows :

The superior officer makes a speech and orders them to obey. The excited crowd, accustomed to be duped by those in high places, understands not a word that the representative of authority is saying in his official, conventional language, and is by no means pacified.

Whereupon the commanding officer declares that unless they submit and disperse, he will be forced to have recourse to arms. If the crowd still refuses to yield and does not disperse, he orders his men to load the muskets and to fire over their heads, and then, if the peasants still stand their ground, he orders the soldiers to aim at the crowds; they fire, and men fall wounded and killed in the street. The crowd is dispersed, the soldiers, carrying out the orders of their commanders, having laid hands upon those whom they suppose to be the chief instigators, and arrested them.

The dying, stained with blood, the wounded, mutilated, and dead, among whom are often women and children, are picked up. The dead are buried, the wounded sent to the hospitals. Those who are supposed to be the ringleaders are taken to the city and court-martialed, and if proved that they have used violence, they are summarily hung.

This has happened in Russia repeatedly, and similar scenes must take place wherever the system of government is based upon violence. Such is the course adopted in cases of revolt.

If, on the other hand, the peasants submit :

The Governor, on his arrival at the place, either quarters the soldiers in the different houses of the village, where their maintenance ruins the peasants

Or, satisfied by threatening the people, he graciously pardons them and departs.

Or, as more frequently happens, he addresses the multitude, upbraids them for disobedience, and announces that the ringleaders must be punished ; he seizes a certain number of men considered as such, and without any form of trial causes them to be beaten with rods in his presence.

In order to give an idea of the manner in which such an affair is conducted, I will describe an instance of the kind which happened in Orel, which was approved by the higher authorities. Like the landowner in Tula, the landed proprietor at Orel chose to take possession of the peasants' property, and here, too, as in the former instance, the peasants resisted. In this case, the landowner, without the consent of the peasants, wished to dam up, for the benefit of his mill, a flow of water which supplied the meadows. The peasants resisted this.

The landlord lodged a complaint with the rural commissary, who illegally (as was afterward admitted by the court) decided the case in favor of the landowner, giving him leave to divert the water. The landowner sent workmen to close the channel through which the water descended. The peasants, excited at this unfair judgment, sent their women to prevent the landowner's men from damming the channel. The women proceeded to the dam, upset the carts, and drove the workmen away. The landowner entered a complaint against them for committing a lawless act. The rural commissary gave the order to arrest and lock up in the village jail one woman out of every family,—an order rather difficult to execute, since each family included several women; and as it was impossible to tell which of them to arrest, the police could not fulfil the order. The landowner complained to the Governor of the laxity of the police.

The Governor, without stopping to consider the case, gave strict orders to the Chief police officer to carry out at once the orders of the rural commissary. In obedience to his superior, the Chief police officer arrived in the village, and with that contempt for the individual peculiar to Russian authorities, ordered the police to seize the first women they could. Disputes and resistance arose.

The Chief police officer, paying no attention to this, persisted in his order that the police should take one woman, innocent or guilty, from every household, and put her under arrest. The peasants defended their wives and mothers; they refused to give them up, and resisted the police and the Chief police officer.

Thus another and a greater offense was committed, —resistance to authority, —which was at once reported in town. Then the Governor, just as I saw the Governor of Tula, with a battalion of soldiers supplied with rods and muskets, backed by all due accessories of telegraph and telephone, accompanied by a learned physician who was to superintend the flogging from a medical standpoint, started on an express train for the spot, like the modern Genghis Khan predicted by Herzen.

In the administration building were the soldiers, a detachment of police with their revolvers suspended on red cords, the principal peasants of the neighbourhood, and the men accused. Around them had collected a crowd of perhaps a thousand.

Driving up to this group, the Governor alighted from his carriage and delivered an address, which had been prepared in advance, after which he inquired for the criminals, and ordered a bench to be brought. No one understood what he meant until the policeman, who always accompanied the Governor and made all the arrangements for the punishments which had already been enforced several times in the government of Orel, explained that the bench was to be used for flogging. This bench and the rods that had been brought by the party were both produced. The executioners had been previously selected from certain horse-thieves taken from the same village, the military having refused to do the business.

When all was ready the Governor bade the first of the twelve men who were pointed out to him by the landowner as the ringleaders to step forward. It so happened that he was the father of a family, a man forty-five years of age, respected in the community, whose rights he had manfully defended.

He was led to the bench, stripped, and ordered to lie down.

He would have begged for mercy, but realizing how little it would avail, he made the sign of the cross and stretched himself out on the bench. Two policemen held him down, and the learned doctor stood by, ready in case of need to give his scientific assistance. The executioners having spat upon their hands, swung the rods, and the flogging began. The bench, it seemed, was too narrow, and it was found difficult to keep the writhing victim, whose muscles twitched convulsively, from falling off.

Then the Governor ordered to be brought another bench, to which a plank was adjusted in such a way as to support it. The soldiers, ever ready with their continual salutes and responses of "Yes, your Excellency," swiftly and obediently executed the orders, while in the meantime the half-naked, pale, and suffering man, trembling, with contracted brows and downcast eyes, stood by waiting. When the bench was readjusted, he was again stretched out upon it, and the horse-stealers renewed their blows. His back, his legs, and even his sides were covered with bleeding wounds, and every blow was followed by the muffled groan which he could no longer repress. In the crowd that stood by one could hear the sobs of the wife and mother, the children, and the kinsfolk of the man, as well as of all who had been called to witness the punishment.

The wretched Governor, intoxicated with power, who had no doubt convinced himself of the necessity for this performance, counted the strokes on his fingers, while he smoked cigarette after cigarette, for the lighting of which several obliging persons hastened to offer him a burning match.

After fifty blows had been given, the peasant lay motionless, without uttering a sound, and the doctor, who had been educated in a government school that he might devote his scientific knowledge to the service of his country and his sovereign, approached the tortured man, felt his pulse, listened to the beating of his heart, and reported to the representative of authority that the victim had become unconscious, and declared that, from a scientific point of view, it might prove dangerous to prolong the punishment.

But the unfortunate Governor, utterly intoxicated by the sight of blood, ordered the flogging to go on until seventy strokes had been given, the number which he for some reason deemed necessary. After the seventieth blow the Governor said:—
"That will do! Now bring on the next one!"

They raised the mutilated and unconscious man, with his swollen back, and carried him away, and the next was brought forward. The sobs and groans of the crowd increased, but the tortures were continued.

So it went on until each of the twelve men had received seventy strokes. They begged for mercy, they groaned and screamed. The sobs and moans of the women grew louder and more heartrending, and the faces of the men of the crowd more gloomy. But there stood the troops, and the torture did not cease until it had seemed sufficient to the unfortunate, half-intoxicated, erring man called the Governor.

Not only did the magistrates, the officers, and the soldiers sanction this act by their presence, but they took part in it, prevent-

ing the crowd from interfering with the order of its execution.

When I asked one of the chief officials why these tortures were inflicted after the men had already submitted, he replied, with the significant air of a man who understands all the fine points of political wisdom, that it was done because it had been proved by experience that if the peasants are not punished they will soon begin again to oppose the decrees of authority, and that the punishment of a few strengthens forever the power of authority.

And now I saw the Governor of Tula, with his clerks, officers, and soldiers, on his way to perform a similar act. Once more by murder or torture the sentence of the higher authorities was to be carried out,—a sentence whose object was to enable a young landowner, the possessor of a yearly income of 100,000 roubles, to receive 3000 roubles more from a tract of forest of which he had basely defrauded a whole community of needy and starving peasants for

This money he would then squander in a few weeks in the restaurants of St. Petersburg, Moscow, and Paris.

Such was the errand of the men I met.

WHAT IS COMMUNISM AND SOCIALISM ?

Here are some videos to briefly explain

https://youtu.be/FrtDZ-LOXFw

https://youtu.be/UhEkJ4noN68

In short, communism promises a world of equality without the injustice of class differences. Such as the rich oppressing the poor for example

The promises of communism is very attractive, I too hope for such a world

But the main problem of communism is Karl Marx's advocacy for the use of violence to achieve those goals

Its like Karl Marx proposing that we can build a beautiful loving family by getting married and having children

And we ask : What if no one wants to marry us ?

Karl Marx replies : You can take them by force and make them bear your children

Do you think a beautiful loving family can be the result ?

What happens in communist / socialist takeovers, is that a group
of privileged people will use Marxist Communist Socialist ideas
to rouse the poor majority to rise up violently against the exist-
ing establishment

But then after the dust settles, these select privilieged few them-
sleves become the elite in their society and begin to subject
the poor to their new brand of oppression. The results are often
worse than before with countless deaths.

Hence the unending cycle of suffering continues

Its like relying on drugs which cause cancer to cure cancer, would
cancer diminish ?

Or to use a cloth soiled with dung to wipe the dining table someone vomited on, would you dine on this table after ?
Having said all the above, of course I condemn the pre existent
conditions of social oppression as outlined in Leo Tolstoy's story
above

Which is why it is now time that we finally work on a solution to
these problems

THE PROBLEM OF COMMUNISM

The problem of communism is illustrated by this scenario :

Lets assume 1000 students took an exam and these are the results

100 students got the high score of 80% and above

200 students got the score of 70%

200 students got the score of 50%

200 students got the score of 40%

200 students got the score of 30%

100 students got the score of 20% and below

Suddenly the school declares : Those who score higher than 50 marks will need to redistribute your points to other students who score lower than 50 marks

That way all students can be equal !

Those who refuse will be beaten up or worse !

300 students score 50% above

700 students score 50% below

The 700 students rejoiced because now they can get additional marks to make up for their lack

The 300 students who score more than 50% began to question what is the exam for in the first place ?

They even start to think, why should they work so hard then if its just going to be taken away by force ?

What is the purpose of exam ? What is the purpose of school ?

From the 300 students, those who could get pass the school guards by climbing the walls left

The rest studied just enough to get the score of 50% and thats it

This is what communism does

An old soviet joke : So long as the bosses pretend to pay us, we will pretend to work

And this is what I heard happened in early days of Communist

China:

When the authorities began to take away huge amounts of crop harvest from productive farmers

These farmers began to eat their crops when they are still not ripe yet

Its called 吃青

Long story short, food supply dwindled, many people died of starvation

WHAT IS CAPITALISM AND THE FREE MARKET ?

Here are some videos to briefly explain

https://youtu.be/fJr2RO7g7jI

https://youtu.be/Fdfru9NHGvE

https://youtu.be/7_7Jv2oh9s4

https://youtu.be/SYOV8XVsX1U

https://youtu.be/4DxXHh-p-O4

In short, Free Market is the voluntary exchange of goods between people without intervention from any third party

However I dont agree that the free market exists in the world today
To search for a pure and truly free market economy would be like searching for a unicorn because of one thing and one thing alone – **EVIL exists**

In all democratic "capitalistic" nations today as far as I know, practice at least 3 tenets out of the 10 tenets of Communism as outlined in The Communist Manifesto (Page 65) https://www.gutenberg.org/ebooks/23905

Namely :

1) A heavily progressive or graduated income tax is enforced.

2) Control of currency is centralised by the country's central bank hence can be manipulated at whim

3) Communication is centralised through censorship and suppression of alternative media

All these factors hold influence over the people's livelihood, directly or indirectly

So in actuality, "Democratic capitalistic" countries are in fact democratic frameworks encroached with elements of communism. And submerged within this superstructure is the market which is forced to navigate the external coercions imposed by Marxist ideology (Communism / Socialism)

The difference between a Democratic country with socialistic elements VS a Communist country with capitalistic elements, is the basis from which its built upon

Democracy is founded and based on choice, the idea that people should have the right to choose how things are done on a collective level

So the potential for political change is at least promised but of course the fulfilment of the promise greatly depends on a variety of factors

On the other hand, **Socialism** is the pathway to **Communism.** And as prescribed by Marx himself, **Communism** can only be achieved through violent force, only those with sufficient might and brutality have the right to decide how things are done on a collective level.

Because of this, the potential for peaceful political change in an openly **Communist / Socialist** country is very difficult but hopefully not impossible

No other political system in the world gives room for peaceful political change, except Democracy

This contributes a big part to why its the best political system in the world

THE PROBLEM OF DEMOCRACY

The big problem of democracy because to choose to have democracy as a political system just means that you choose to have the right to choose !

It is as funny as it sounds XD

Yes the people have the right to choose but choose between what ?

And how can people make right political choices if they dont even make right choices in their own life ?

While communism, socialism and other -isms have seemingly clear cut directions

Democracy is similar to a sandbox in a way

This can be a good thing and a bad thing

Lets not forget the reason why most Democratic countries in the world have elements of communism is because the **people voted such policies in**

In other words, the majority **voted to use the threat of violent force to make the minority comply to their will**

And recently its more and more apparent that a lot of democracies are actually controlled by a "deep state"

A deep state is a network of unelected officials within the government exerting actual control over the country

This makes legally elected officials mere figureheads and the democratic election process merely a show

To address this problem we must first examine, what is the government ?

WHAT IS THE GOVERNMENT ?

The government itself does not exist in the physical world

Yes we can see government buildings but to say that a government building is the government would be to say that a religious building is God

Or to say that the Earth is gravity

The Government is a **metaphysical idea** in the minds of man which has real world consequences because ideas have consequences in reality

The Government is a metaphysical entity which defines right and wrong through the laws it enforces on the people under its control

The Government is an idea which controls the people but who controls the Government ?

That is politics

The peculiarities of the Government is that whoever wields it gains the power to define right and wrong, good and evil in the midst of society

Example,

A robber who takes from you against your will, its called robbery

When Caesar takes from you against your will, its called taxation

A person kills someone, he is a murderer

When Caesar kills someone, he is a warrior

The list goes on but I think you get the gist

The Government is the metaphysical instrument which has monopoly over the use of force

Therefore whoever gains the wielding right to this instrument gains exception to the rules imposed on the rest of society

That is why its so dangerous to have a big pervasive government ruling over society

Because evil people would do anything to wield this instrument over others

There is a saying : Power corrupts and absolute power corrupts absolutely

Even if a decent person comes to power and wields the power of Government, the odds are that they will be swept along with the flow of corruption as well

On top of that, because the government is run as a top down hierarchal system, it inherits the problems of hierarchy as outlined here
https://famecherry.com/society/hierarchy

The problems of the hierarchy system infects all political systems

Example :

Politician A was voted into power and spent tons of money and pocketed lots of it, country goes into debt, who ends up paying the bil ?

Politician B was then voted into power to fix problems caused by **Politician A.** Taxes were raised to service the debt incurred, so in other words, the people pays for the bill incurred by Politician A

1) Why does **Politician B** need to fix issues caused by **Politician A** ?

2) Why does the people need to pay for the debts incurred by **Politician A** ?

3) Why not **Politician A** pay for the debts he incurred ?

4) Why not those who voted **Politician A** into office pay for the debts incurred ?

Long story short, the problem of hierarchy is the lack of individual responsibility

Despite of this, **Democracy is still the best** because at least you get the chance to make a peaceful transition of power

In all other political systems you get the same problems but no way to peacefully change the power structure

In a democracy, the political choices available at the ballot box generally reflects the maturity of the population at large

The more educated and well informed the public is, the better choices they get when the time to vote comes

However optimistic this sounds, we must not forget, **<u>EVIL exists</u>**

The education system and media at large is generally fine tuned to ensure that people's maturity stays as low as possible so that evil people can come to power or stay in power

Logic and reason helps democratic countries get better and better, therefore, **<u>EVIL people</u>** target logic and reason itself

These are the challenges that democratic countries face today

THE SOLUTION

The solution to Capitalism vs Communism is also the solution to politics

I discovered this solution through being an analogue camera film trader

You can check out my full story here
https://famecherry.com/society/film-economy

A short conclusion of the story is as follows

The film market operates on a relatively free economy model with minimal external interference except import tax

The price for film goods dont naturally go down because its not a natural tendency to want to sell as cheap as possible, the usual practice is to sell as high as the market ceiling allows in order to maximise profit

As a film seller, my business is run based on divine principles and purpose. As a result, I sell cheaper and have more ready stock variety than any seller in the market in Malaysia.

Film became more accessible than ever here in Malaysia. So much so that even people from Singapore, Vietnam, Brunei,

Thailand and even South Korea buy from me. Some even to re-sell in their own market.

As overseas demand for the goods are high, sometimes I am tempted to one shot sell off all my goods overseas and get the profit immediately. But I did not do that, because I know that the availability of local film stock influences the demand for film processing and camera repair as well, there are people whose livelihood depends on this. I aim to always ensure adequate quantity of stock to keep the local market running.

As I know that my price is much lower than the market price, I chose to sell mainly from my website and not intrude into marketplaces like Shopee and Lazada because I know there are people whose livelihood depends on this as well.

Plus also I know that the more film sellers are in the market the better for the growth of the analogue film community, so its best if all film sellers can be good team players to serve the community at large.

All this I have done without need of some regulatory law to tell me how to run my business

The problem with the free market is that, the market won't change by itself, it still takes someone to step up to influence the market in a positive way

Hence, the solution is to ensure a free market economy on the external and run a self-controlled market economy on the internal

*In other words, the solution is **<u>to maintain the freedom to buy</u>***

<u>and sell freely according to supply and demand BUT on the internal, the seller sets the price based on internal principles and the purpose for doing the business</u>

So it's internally enforced principles and purpose which serve as the controlled part of the economy

And because control comes from the internal, there is no need for an external dictator to tell the seller what price to sell

It's important to avoid having external dictators because they usually have no technical idea about the film market nor care about the people involved in the market itself and probably has never ever run a day of honest business on his own before

He is just doing what is popular to the people in the short term to stay in power without thinking much about the long term re-percussions

By striving to maintain a free external market economy whenever possible but maintain an economy controlled by divine principles within our hearts, external dictators shall have no place in society

This is the solution !

To translate the solution into political terms

By striving to **maintain Democracy as much as possible on the outside but maintain a Theocracy within our hearts** is the solution

Evil people will have no excuse to solicit that we give sovere-

ignity of ourselves over to them the moment all of us are able
to govern our individual lives properly through partnership with
the Creator Himself

Specifically, it is only the Theocracy of Jesus which solves the problem of politics because of its unique nuances, namely :

> **2000 years ago, King Jesus came unto us, inherits His Kingdom, was killed then resurrected and leaves us with specific instructions to teach the whole world His ways**
>
> **Then He departs from this world and leaves us with the Holy Spirit to flesh out His Royal Majesty's instructions**
>
> **Part of His instructions includes His promise of sudden return to this world to render judgement unto all, and also that we make no images of Him here as per the original constitution of His Kingdom passed down by His Father**

There is nothing in the world like this. On the surface this seems counterintuitive on so many levels but when put into practice we get a Monarchy on Earth in which the King is away but may return suddenly anytime

We get decentralisation on a material level but direct centralisation on an immaterial level as we connect directly with our King through the Holy Spirit to do His Royal Majesty's work, without needing any third parties such as bureaucrats or priests

I will flesh out this thought more in future works

There is no other path to freedom but this

DIVINE LAW

These are the laws of God which act as the antidote to Communism

The Sabbatic Year

"At the end of every seven years you shall grant a remission of debts. "This is the manner of remission: every creditor shall release what he has loaned to his neighbor; he shall not exact it of his neighbor and his brother, because the LORD'S remission has been proclaimed. "From a foreigner you may exact it, but your hand shall release whatever of yours is with your brother. "However, there will be no poor among you, since the LORD will surely bless you in the land which the LORD your God is giving you as an inheritance to possess, if only you listen obediently to the voice of the LORD your God, to observe carefully all this commandment which I am commanding you today. "For the LORD your God will bless you as He has promised you, and you will lend to many nations, but you will not borrow; and you will rule over many nations, but they will not rule over you.

"If there is a poor man with you, one of your brothers, in any of your towns in your land which the LORD your God is giving you, you shall not harden your heart, nor close your hand from your poor brother; but you shall freely open your hand to him, and shall generously lend him sufficient for his need in what-

ever he lacks. "Beware that there is no base thought in your heart, saying, 'The seventh year, the year of remission, is near,' and your eye is hostile toward your poor brother, and you give him nothing; then he may cry to the LORD against you, and it will be a sin in you. "You shall generously give to him, and your heart shall not be grieved when you give to him, because for this thing the LORD your God will bless you in all your work and in all your undertakings. "For the poor will never cease to be in the land; therefore I command you, saying, 'You shall freely open your hand to your brother, to your needy and poor in your land.'

"If your kinsman, a Hebrew man or woman, is sold to you, then he shall serve you six years, but in the seventh year you shall set him free. "When you set him free, you shall not send him away empty-handed. "You shall furnish him liberally from your flock and from your threshing floor and from your wine vat; you shall give to him as the LORD your God has blessed you. "You shall remember that you were a slave in the land of Egypt, and the LORD your God redeemed you; therefore I command you this today. "It shall come about if he says to you, 'I will not go out from you,' because he loves you and your household, since he fares well with you; Then you shall take an awl and pierce it through his ear into the door, and he shall be your servant forever. Also you shall do likewise to your maidservant.

"It shall not seem hard to you when you set him free, for he has given you six years with double the service of a hired man; so the LORD your God will bless you in whatever you do.

"You shall consecrate to the LORD your God all the firstborn males that are born of your herd and of your flock; you shall not work with the firstborn of your herd, nor shear the firstborn of your flock. "You and your household shall eat it every year before the LORD your God in the place which the LORD chooses. "But if it has any defect, such as lameness or blindness, or any serious defect, you shall not sacrifice it to the LORD your God.

"You shall eat it within your gates; the unclean and the clean alike may eat it, as a gazelle or a deer. "Only you shall not eat its blood; you are to pour it out on the ground like water.

The Sabbatic Year and Year of Jubilee

You are also to count off seven sabbaths of years for yourself, seven times seven years, so that you have the time of the seven sabbaths of years, namely, forty-nine years. 'You shall then sound a ram's horn abroad on the tenth day of the seventh month; on the day of atonement you shall sound a horn all through your land. 'You shall thus consecrate the fiftieth year and proclaim a release through the land to all its inhabitants. It shall be a jubilee for you, and each of you shall return to his own property, and each of you shall return to his family. 'You shall have the fiftieth year as a jubilee; you shall not sow, nor reap its aftergrowth, nor gather in from its untrimmed vines. 'For it is a jubilee; it shall be holy to you. You shall eat its crops out of the field.

'On this year of jubilee each of you shall return to his own property. 'If you make a sale, moreover, to your friend or buy from your friend's hand, you shall not wrong one another. 'Corresponding to the number of years after the jubilee, you shall buy from your friend; he is to sell to you according to the number of years of crops. 'In proportion to the extent of the years you shall increase its price, and in proportion to the fewness of the years you shall diminish its price, for it is a number of crops he is selling to you. 'So you shall not wrong one another, but you shall fear your God; for I am the LORD your God.

'You shall thus observe My statutes and keep My judgments, so as to carry them out, that you may live securely on the land. 'Then the land will yield its produce, so that you can eat your fill *and live securely on it. 'But if you say, "What are we going to eat on the seventh year if we do not sow or gather in our crops?" then I will so order My blessing for you in the sixth year that it will bring forth the crop for three years. 'When you are sowing the eighth year, you can still eat old things from the crop, eating the old until the ninth year when its crop comes in.*

The Law of Redemption

'The land, moreover, shall not be sold permanently, for the land is Mine; for you are but aliens and sojourners with Me. 24'Thus for every piece of your property, you are to provide for the redemption of the land.

'If a fellow countryman of yours becomes so poor he has to sell part of his property, then his nearest kinsman is to come and buy back what his relative has sold. 'Or in case a man has no kinsman, but so recovers his means as to find sufficient for its redemption, then he shall calculate the years since its sale and refund the balance to the man to whom he sold it, and so return to his property. 'But if he has not found sufficient means to get it back for himself, then what he has sold shall remain in the hands of its purchaser until the year of jubilee; but at the jubilee it shall revert, that he may return to his property.

'Likewise, if a man sells a dwelling house in a walled city, then his redemption right remains valid until a full year from its sale; his right of redemption lasts a full year. 'But if it is not bought back for him within the space of a full year, then the house that is in the walled city passes permanently to its purchaser throughout his generations; it does not revert in the jubilee. 'The houses of the villages, however, which have no surrounding wall shall be considered as open fields; they have redemption rights and revert in the jubilee. 'As for cities of the Levites, the Levites have a permanent right of redemption for the houses of the cities which are their possession. 'What, therefore, belongs to the Levites may be redeemed and a house sale in the city of this possession reverts in the jubilee, for the houses of the cities of the Levites are their possession among the sons of Israel. 'But pasture fields of their cities shall not be sold, for that is their perpetual possession.

<u>**Of Poor Countrymen**</u>

'Now in case a countryman of yours becomes poor and his means with regard to you falter, then you are to sustain him, like a stranger or a sojourner, that he may live with you. 'Do not take usurious interest from him, but revere your God, that your countryman may live with you. 'You shall not give him your silver at interest, nor your food for gain. 'I am the LORD your God, who brought you out of the land of Egypt to give you the land of Canaan and to be your God.

'If a countryman of yours becomes so poor with regard to you that he sells himself to you, you shall not subject him to a slave's service. 'He shall be with you as a hired man, as if he were a sojourner; he shall serve with you until the year of jubilee. 'He shall then go out from you, he and his sons with him, and shall go back to his family, that he may return to the property of his forefathers. 'For they are My servants whom I brought out from the land of Egypt; they are not to be sold in a slave sale. 'You shall not rule over him with severity, but are to revere your God. 'As for your male and female slaves whom you may have—you may acquire male and female slaves from the pagan nations that are around you. 'Then, too, it is out of the sons of the sojourners who live as aliens among you that you may gain acquisition, and out of their families who are with you, whom they will have produced in your land; they also may become your possession. 'You may even bequeath them to your sons after you, to receive as a possession; you can use them as permanent slaves. But in respect to your countrymen, the sons of Israel, you shall not rule with severity over one another.

Of Redeeming a Poor Man

'Now if the means of a stranger or of a sojourner with you becomes sufficient, and a countryman of yours becomes so poor with regard to him as to sell himself to a stranger who is sojourning with you, or to the descendants of a stranger's family, then he shall have redemption right after he has been sold. One of his brothers may redeem him, or his uncle, or his uncle's son, may redeem him, or one of his blood relatives from his family may redeem him; or if he prospers, he may redeem himself. 'He then with his purchaser shall calculate from the year when he sold himself to him up to the year of jubilee; and the price of his sale shall correspond to the number of years. It is like the days of a hired man that he shall be with him. 'If there are still many years, he shall refund part of his purchase price in proportion to them for his own redemption; and if few years remain until the year of jubilee, he shall so calculate with him. In proportion to his years he is to refund the amount for his redemption. 'Like a man hired year by year he shall be with him; he shall not rule over him with severity in your sight. 'Even if he is not redeemed by these means, he shall still go out in the year of jubilee, he and his sons with him. 'For the sons of Israel are My servants; they are My servants whom I brought out from the land of Egypt. I am the Lord your God.

If the law sounds like ancient text to you, you are right. It is ancient text written in an ancient context.

But don't worry, Jesus Christ came so that we may integrate the principles of the above into our lives and universalise these values across the globe !

Below is how Jesus teaches us to perceive the laws of God

"You have heard that it was said to those of old, 'You shall not murder; and whoever murders will be liable to judgment.' But I say to you that everyone who is angry with his brotherc will be liable to judgment; whoever insultsd his brother will be liable to the council; and whoever says, 'You fool!' will be liable to the helle of fire. So if you are offering your gift at the altar and there remember that your brother has something against you, leave your gift there before the altar and go. First be reconciled to your brother, and then come and offer your gift. Come to terms quickly with your accuser while you are going with him to court, lest your accuser hand you over to the judge, and the judge to the guard, and you be put in prison. Truly, I say to you, you will never get out until you have paid the last penny.

***Context** : https://biblehub.com/esv/matthew/5.htm*

Interpretation: The surface text of law is just a guideline, it is the guiding principles behind the law which is what God wants you to live by

The law of God is not to be used to wage legal battle upon others or to oppress others, it's not what it's designed for.

"You have heard that it was said, 'You shall not commit adultery.' But I say to you that everyone who looks at a woman with lustful intent has already committed adultery with her in his heart. If your right eye causes you to sin, tear it out and throw it away. For it is better that you lose one of your members than that your whole body be thrown into hell.And if your right hand causes you to sin, cut it off and throw it away. For it is better that you lose one of your members than that your whole body go into hell.

Context *: https://biblehub.com/esv/matthew/5.htm*

Interpretation : If you read the Law of God for the guiding principles behind them, it can help your problem areas within yourself in which you can nip in the bud so that they won't have a chance to manifest into reality.

You can gain the strength and will to make a change in yourself if you take full ownership of the mistakes you commit instead of just blaming your mistakes on externalities.

Example someone who says : Its not my fault, its my eyes which cause me to peep at a woman bathing ! Or its not my fault, its my hand which cause me to steal !

"You have heard that it was said, 'You shall love your neighbor and hate your enemy.' But I say to you, Love your enemies and pray for those who persecute you, so that you may be sons of your Father who is in heaven. For he makes his sun rise on the evil and on the good, and sends rain on the just and on the unjust. For if you love those who love you, what reward do you have? Do not even the tax collectors do the same? And if you greet only your brothers,i what more are you doing than others? Do not even the Gentiles do the same? You therefore must be perfect, as your heavenly Father is perfect.

***Context** : https://biblehub.com/esv/matthew/5.htm*

"You have heard that it was said, 'An eye for an eye and a tooth for a tooth.' But I say to you, Do not resist the one who is evil. But if anyone slaps you on the right cheek, turn to him the other also. And if anyone would sue you and take your tunic,h let him have your cloak as well. And if anyone forces you to go one mile, go with him two miles. Give to the one who begs from you, and do not refuse the one who would borrow from you.

***Context** : https://biblehub.com/esv/matthew/5.htm*

Interpretation : Jesus nullified the violent parts of the Law both through His teaching and demonstration through His life and death on the cross.

Jesus's resurrection is the mark of God's approval upon Him.

And he said to them, "The Sabbath was made for man, not man for the Sabbath. 28So the Son of Man is lord even of the Sabbath."

__Context__ : https://biblehub.com/esv/mark/2.htm

Interpretation : The Law of God is not designed to be a system to be worshipped so that man serves the Law but the other way around

The Law is designed to serve man so that man may understand the heart of God through understanding the principles behind God's law

"Judge not, and you will not be judged; condemn not, and you will not be condemned; forgive, and you will be forgiven; give, and it will be given to you. Good measure, pressed down, shaken together, running over, will be put into your lap. For with the measure you use it will be measured back to you."

He also told them a parable: "Can a blind man lead a blind man? Will they not both fall into a pit? A disciple is not above his teacher, but everyone when he is fully trained will be like his teacher. Why do you see the speck that is in your brother's eye, but do not notice the log that is in your own eye? How can you say to your brother, 'Brother, let me take out the speck that is in your eye,' when you yourself do not see the log that is in your own eye? You hypocrite, first take the log out of your own eye, and then you will see clearly to take out the speck that is in your brother's eye.

Context *: https://biblehub.com/esv/luke/6.htm*

Interpretation : The Law of God is not designed to be used to judge and condemn others

Before we begin to tell someone their error, we should first begin by examining ourselves and fix our own errors first

"Judge not, that you be not judged. For with the judgment you pronounce you will be judged, and with the measure you use it will be measured to you. Why do you see the speck that is in your brother's eye, but do not notice the log that is in your own eye? Or how can you say to your brother, 'Let me take the speck out of your eye,' when there is the log in your own eye? You hypocrite, first take the log out of your own eye, and then you will see clearly to take the speck out of your brother's eye.

"Do not give dogs what is holy, and do not throw your pearls before pigs, lest they trample them underfoot and turn to attack you.

Context *: https://biblehub.com/esv/matthew/7.htm*

Interpretation : The Law of God is not designed to be imposed upon those who do not follow the Law of God

THE CONSTITUTION
OF FREEDOM

The Divine Law above is actually just a small portion from a whole framework that God gave us

After almost two years, I have organised the framework into categories so that they may be integrated more easily within us

Behold, the Constitution of Freedom
https://famecherry.com/constitution

Its no doubt that as more people live with God's divine law alive in their hearts, the world will change

Lets not forget that the **Garden of Eden was here on Earth**

A river flowed out of Eden to water the garden, and there it divided and became four rivers. The name of the first is the Pishon. It is the one that flowed around the whole land of Havilah, where there is gold. And the gold of that land is good; bdellium and onyx stone are there. The name of the second river is the Gihon. It is the one that flowed around the whole land of Cush. And the name of the third river is the Tigris, which flows east of Assyria. And the fourth river is the Euphrates.

Context : *https://biblehub.com/esv/genesis/2.htm*

Eden was the place where once God walked with man. So by that definition, Heaven. Paradise.

But when Adam and Eve ate from the tree of the knowledge of good & evil, they took the power to define good and evil for themselves. To define right and wrong by their own definition instead of God's.

Therefore they were cast out from Eden.

But God out of His mercy and kindness, sent His own begotten son Jesus unto us. So that together with Jesus, we may bring Eden into the world.

The kingdom of God cometh not with observation: Neither shall they say, Lo here! or, lo there! for, behold, the kingdom of God is within you.

Context : *https://biblehub.com/kjv/luke/17.htm*

Interpretation : By internalising and living out God's principles, Eden flows out from our hearts to our hands and from our hands to the people around us in the world

The kingdom of heaven is like a grain of mustard seed that a man took and sowed in his field. It is the smallest of all seeds, but when it has grown it is larger than all the garden plants and becomes a tree, so that the birds of the air come and make nests in its branches."

The kingdom of heaven is like leaven that a woman took and hid in three measures of flour, till it was all leavened."

Context : https://biblehub.com/esv/matthew/13.htm

Interpretation : Because each and everyone one of us are uniquely designed with different gifts, abilities and talent given by God, even if we have the same principles living within us, the manifestation into reality would be different and uniquely reflective of our original design as well.

The process of transforming Earth into Eden occurs not just on one place alone but in an asymmetric even way all the nations at once, slowly but surely. Therefore like leaven unto a dough.

In short, through Jesus, we now can gain the ability to stop defining right and wrong for ourselves but to make the choice to define right and wrong by God's standards instead.

Look at the problems of the world today, its all because man choose to define good and evil for themselves and to impose these definitions on others.

This will not stop until the message of Jesus is preached unto all the ends of the world.

"See that no one leads you astray. For many will come in my name, saying, 'I am the Christ,' and they will lead many astray. And you will hear of wars and rumors of wars. See that you are not alarmed, for this must take place, but the end is not yet. For nation will rise against nation, and kingdom against kingdom, and there will be famines and earthquakes in various places. All these are but the beginning of the birth pains.

"Then they will deliver you up to tribulation and put you to death, and you will be hated by all nations for my name's sake. And then many will fall away and betray one another and hate one another. And many false prophets will arise and lead many astray. And because lawlessness will be increased, the love of many will grow cold. But the one who endures to the end will be saved. And this gospel of the kingdom will be proclaimed throughout the whole world as a testimony to all nations, and then the end will come.

Context : https://biblehub.com/esv/matthew/24.htm

Therefore I say unto you, Take no thought for your life, what ye shall eat, or what ye shall drink; nor yet for your body, what ye shall put on. Is not the life more than meat, and the body than raiment? Behold the fowls of the air: for they sow not, neither do they reap, nor gather into barns; yet your heavenly Father feedeth them. Are ye not much better than they? Which of you by taking thought can add one cubit unto his stature? 28And why take ye thought for raiment? Consider the lilies of the field, how they grow; they toil not, neither do they spin: And yet I say unto you, That even Solomon in all his glory was not arrayed like one of these. Wherefore, if God so clothe the grass of the field, which to day is, and to morrow is cast into the oven, shall he not much more clothe you, O ye of little faith? Therefore take no thought, saying, What shall we eat? or, What shall we drink? or, Wherewithal shall we be clothed? (For after all these things do the Gentiles seek:) for your heavenly Father knoweth that ye have need of all these things.

But seek ye first the kingdom of God, and his righteousness; and all these things shall be added unto you.

Take therefore no thought for the morrow: for the morrow shall take thought for the things of itself. Sufficient unto the day is the evil thereof.

Context *: https://biblehub.com/kjv/matthew/6.htm*

Interpretation : By prioritising God's definition of right and wrong in the running of our lives, our needs in reality will fall into place by itself

In a common sense way its also because we will spend less time trying to victimise others and more time actually tackling the real issues at hand instead

Plus people who share this vision generally have super awesome teamwork due to having a work excellence driven by divine purpose

Even if we just follow the logical pathways to understand what money, sex and health is , they all lead to this path

Know The Logic Behind What Money Is

– https://famecherry.com/money

And know that True wealth is people

Know The Logic Behind What Sex Is

– https://famecherry.com/sex

And know that its for making people

Know The Logic Behind What Makes Good Health

– https://famecherry.com/health

And know to have good health requires a driven purpose in people

And what helps people stop constantly victimising one another ?

The principles as described here in this book is what helps

The True indication of a healthy society and nation is

1) Genuine trust amongst each other (Because people stop victimising one another)

2) Organic population growth (Because men and women trust each other)

3) Indigenous growth of capital in the form of tools and expertise (Because parents raise their children properly hence imparting knowledge into the future effectively)

GDP is just a measure of superficial things which are heavily manipulated anyway

The above is what really counts

I really hope my work can help reconcile society which is now being more and more polarised and fractured

This is what would help heal the world, I lay this down upon your feet for your consideration

My hope is a better future for my children and your children

Nevertheless, the Kingdom of God shall advance

Alleluia